Mits and the Van

By Debbie Croft

"Mits," said Tim.

"Kel is in the van."

Wag, wag!

Tim and Mits run to the van.

Mits can see lots of kids!

"Sit, Mits!" said Tim.

"No dogs at the van!"

Tim gets to Kel.

Mits gets to the van!

"No, Mits!" said Tim.

"Sit, Mits!" said Kel.

But Mits did not sit!

Mits ran to the van.

Lots of kids ran, too!

Tim was mad at Mits.

"Sit, Mits!" said Tim.

Mits sat at the van.

But Kel was not mad.

She fed Mits.

Kel fed Tim, too!

Wag, wag!

CHECKING FOR MEANING

1. What does Tim tell Mits to do by the van? *(Literal)*

2. How does Kel help Mits and Tim? *(Literal)*

3. Why do you think dogs are not allowed at the van? *(Inferential)*

EXTENDING VOCABULARY

van	Look at the word *van*. What smaller word can you see at the end of *van*? What words do you know that rhyme with *van*?
wag	The word *wag* means to move quickly back and forth. What do dogs wag? What else can you think of that can wag?
dogs	Find the base of the word *dogs*. How has adding *s* changed the meaning of the word? What other words in the book have *s* added to the base?

MOVING BEYOND THE TEXT

1. What was Tim buying from the van? What else might people buy from a van?

2. What is your favourite place to go for a walk? What can you see there?

3. Why is it important that dogs are well trained?

4. What other animals can be trained?

SPEED SOUNDS

Kk	Ll	Vv	Qq	Ww		
Dd	Jj	Oo	Gg	Uu		
Cc	Bb	Rr	Ee	Ff	Hh	Nn
Mm	Ss	Aa	Pp	Ii	Tt	

PRACTICE WORDS

Kel

van

wag

kids

lots

Lots

Wag